Why has postcolonial theory forgotten India's Islamic past?
Selected writings of Raja Rammohun Roy (1772-1833):
Recuperating a Hindu-Islamic métissage identity

RAJA RAMMOHUN ROY.

THIS TEXT HAS BEEN COMPILED BY:

OPEN WINDOWS: A FEMINIST RESEARCH
CENTER, BANGALORE, INDIA.

Published by

LIES AND BIG FEET

ISBN: 9384281107
ISBN-13: 978-9384281106

ACKNOWELDGEMENTS.

Identities are in a state of constant flux; they are also social constructs. This text has been written in the hope that we all realize that we live in social systems which desire to codify fixed identities, and thereby, trap us within structures that do not necessarily benefit us.

ACKNOWLEDGMENTS

CONTENTS

PREFATORY NOTE.

Postcolonial theory assumes that European colonization in the last two centuries can be understood within binaries of: colonized-ruler, center-periphery, hegemonic-dominant/ margins, and that these can be the only referential frameworks within which the engagement between the colonial powers and the colonies can be examined. In this process, we tend to erase the pre-colonial pasts, and the heterogeneity which would have been a norm within the colonial societies. In our haste to erase the influence that Islam has had on the Indian psyche, we have arrived at a skewered notion of identity. If we look at the writings of Raja Rammohun Roy (1772-1833), we realize that it was not unusual for educated Hindus to be also trained in Islamic theology. Rammohun's first work, a treatise in Persian (with an Arabic preface), titled *Tuhfat-ul-Muwahhidin, or, A Gift to Monotheists* was a critique of Hindu idolatory, and was written in an abstruse style, and made use of neo-platonic, Arab logic and philosophy. The causal connection is very interesting; Islamic theology comprises part of Rammohun's education and he simultaneously uses it to critique Islam and Hinduism. Does this imply that most Hindus would have been familiar with an Islamic Other, a fact that was erased from their psyches once the Britishers arrived in India ?

By the time of Sir William Jones (1746-1794), England had become an increasingly print-oriented society, shifting away from its oral past. This explains Jones' feverish desire to transcribe every manuscript into print, as the process would lend an element of fixity to unstable scribal texts. In an advertisement in *The Calcutta Gazette*, in 1789, Sir William Jones wrote:

> The correctness of modern Arabian and Persian Books is truly deplorable, nothing can preserve them in any degree of accuracy but the art of printing; and if Asiatic literature should ever be general, it must diffuse itself, as Greek learning was diffused in Italy after the taking of Constantinople, by mere impressions of the best manuscripts without versions or comments, which future scholars would add at their leisure to future editions: but no printer should engage in so expensive a business without the patronage and the purse of monarchs of states, or society of wealthy individuals or at least without a large public subscription.[1]

Jones was extremely conscious of entering a realm of scribal culture in Bengal, and this is reflected in his desire to constantly transfer manuscripts into printed texts. In a way, by transferring written texts into print, his central aim was to codify knowledge, and in the process allow for control of what was disseminated about India

---

[1] William Jones, *The Calcutta Gazette*, October 29, 1789.

SECTION I:
Rammohun's Islamic-Hindu background.

1 THE ISLAMIC IDENTITY WITHIN RAMMOHUN'S BRAHMANICAL LINEAGE.

We do not have records or personal anecdotes of what it meant for a Brahmin in the eighteenth century to work and interact, socially or professionally, with the Britishers. Was this interaction fraught with a sense of racial otherness? It would be rather reductive to write off any relationship between the natives and the Englishmen as one that was between the white ruler and the ruled. In the pre-colonial past, many Brahmins had worked for the Muslim rulers without losing their caste; in fact, they had learnt Persian, which was the language of the court, and acquired Persianised social habits that were in conformity with the ruling class. In a similar vein, working for the British would not really have been socially difficult. The life of Rammohun and his forefathers who worked for the Muslim rulers explains how so many Hindus were able to interact with the British with relative ease. Social interaction of this kind made it possible for the easy transmission of European culture and knowledge into India.

Rammohun was born in 1772 (many regard his date of birth as 1774), in Radhanagar, near Krishnanagar, in a devout Hindu family and inherited the religiosity that marked his forefathers.[2] Krishnanagar was known to be steeped in Hindu culture. His forefathers settled in Murshidabad and were in the service of the Muslim rulers. He wrote in a letter, "My ancestors were Brahmins of a high order, and from time immemorial, were devoted to the religious duties of their race, down to my fifth progenitor who about one hundred and forty years ago gave up spiritual exercises for worldly pursuits and aggrandizement."[3] His forefathers would have known Persian and Urdu. Rammohun's great grandfather, Krishnachandra Banerji, moved his family to the village of Radhanagar, opposite Krishnanagar, and worked for the Nawab of Bengal and earned the title of "Roy". This took place in the reign of Aurangzeb (1619-1707). His youngest son, Brajabinode, was placed in a high position in the court of Siraj-ud-daulah. Eventually, he left the service of the Nawab and retired. His fifth son, Ramkanta, was Rammohun's father. Ramkanta, despite being a Vaishnava, was married to a Sakta. Rammohun's maternal family belonged to the "sacerdotal order by profession as well as by birth ...[and] adhered to a life of religious observances

---

[2] For the life of Rammohun Roy, see Sophia Dobson Collet, *The Life and Letters of Raja Rammohun Roy*, ed. Dilip Kumar Biswas and Prabhat Chandra Ganguli (Calcutta: Sadharon Brahmo Samaj, 1900). Reprint 1988.

[3] "Letter by Rammohun Roy" published by Mr. Sandford Arnot in the *Athenaeum* in London, Oct. 5, 1833, pp. 666-668; quoted in Collet, *Raja Rammohun Roy*, p. 461.

and devotion."[4] His family was equally conversant with the ostentation of the Muslim court and the religiosity of the Hindu temple.

As a young man, Rammohun was educated in Bengali, and later Persian as the latter was the official language. We can speculate that his education would have been a model of how many young men would have been educated. He was sent to Patna to learn Arabic, where he was taught from Arabic translations of Euclid and Aristotle, the Koran, and the writings of the Sufis. Subsequently, he studied Sanskrit at Benares. About this period he wrote:

> In conformity with the usage of my paternal race, and the wish of my father, I studied the Persian and Arabic languages, these being indispensable to those who attached themselves to the courts of the Mohamaden princes, and agreeably to the usage of my maternal relations, I devoted myself to the study of the Sanskrit and the theological works written in it, which contain the body of Hindoo literature, law and religion.[5]

He studied in five different languages, namely, Sanskrit, Arabic, Persian, Urdu and Bengali. The Sanskrit and the Arabic systems of education were very different from each

[4] Ibid., p. 461.

[5] Ibid., p. 461.

other, but each is seen as indispensable to the other. Rammohun reveals remarkable ease in how he was able to master these two varied systems of knowledge. If he was able to comprehend, simultaneously, two different epistemic systems, it is not surprising that subsequently he grasped the revolutionary characteristics of European, modern knowledge. Brajendranath Seal[6] and Sushobhan Sarkar[7] agree that Rammohun's greatness lies in the fact that he was able to synthesize Hindu, Islamic and Western cultures. Reverend William Yates, who was attached to the Baptist missionary wrote a letter in 1816, describing Rammohun:

> I was introduced to him about a year ago; before this, he was not acquainted with anyone who cared for his soul. ... When I first knew him he would talk only on metaphysical subjects such as the eternity of matter ... but he has lately become much more humble and disposed to converse about the Gospel. ... He visited Eustace lately and stayed to family prayer, with which he was quite delighted.[8]

---

[6] Brajendranath Seal, *Rammohun the Universal Man* (Calcutta: Sadharon Brahmo Samaj, 1933), pp.2-3.

[7] Susobhan Chandra Sarkar, *Notes on the Bengal Renaissance* (Bombay: Peoples Publishing House, 1946).

[8] Collet, *Raja Rammohun Roy*, p. 123.

Within a short period of time, as a result of his intimacy with the reverend Rammohun was able to learn about Christianity as it was practised. Rammohun's life allows us to understand how English thought processes were able to impress Indians, as the social and intellectual life of certain sections of India was always receptive to new ideas.

2 Postcolonial theory?

The Koran and the tenets of monotheism made an impact on Rammohun. By the age of fifteen he was critical of idolatory and left home, traveling to Tibet in order to learn about Buddhism. On his return home after a few years, around 1791-92, he was unable to reconcile himself to the beliefs of his family, and had theological disagreements with them. About this period he wrote:

> I proceeded on my travels, and passed through different countries, chiefly within, but some beyond, the bounds of Hindoostan, with a feeling of great aversion to the establishment of the British power in India. When I had reached the age of twenty, my father recalled me, and restored me to his favor; after which I first saw and began to associate with Europeans, and soon after made myself tolerably acquainted with their laws and forms of Government. Finding them generally more intelligent, more steady and moderate in their conduct, I gave up my prejudice against them and

became inclined in their favor.[9]

Within his lifetime, we see the disappearance of one system of life and the emergence of the new. In the early years of his life, the British were still to establish themselves as the rulers of India; more importantly, Rammohun was yet to fully understand the nature of European knowledge. It was only when he started associating with different officials of the East India Company that he realized the modern-ness of Western civilization. By 1796 he had separated from his family, and stayed for a while in Calcutta. He also purchased property in Hooghly, which gave him a steady income. As a result of his moneylending practice he interacted with many officials of the East India Company. He left Calcutta in 1799 and traveled in north India, spending some time in Benares. He studied Sanskrit, and earned a living by copying manuscripts. His father died in 1803 and by 1805, he had started working for the East India Company as a *munshi* in Rangpur; his employer was John Digby. It was here that he started to have socio-religious discussions with his native friends. By 1814, when he moved to Calcutta, he had amassed enough money to become a zamindar that allowed him an annual income of ten thousand rupees.[10] His wealth and his moneylending made him superficially indistinguishable from many of the *zamindars* who lived in Calcutta.

---

[9] "Letter," quoted in Collet, *Raja Rammohun Roy*, p. 462.

[10] For details on his life, see Collet, *Raja Rammohun Roy*, pp. 1-27.

Rammohun, though, was different from his contemporaries. By the time he was twenty, he had broken away from the religious tradition of his father, and was thoroughly familiar with Hindu, Islamic and Buddhist systems of thought. He had started life with the intention of working for the Muslim rulers in Murshidabad, but realized that the Islamic phase of Indian history was on the wane. Rammohun himself had been deeply rooted in the cosmopolitan upper class Persian culture of the eighteenth century[11] but with the consolidation of British power in India, Rammohun and many of his generation of the early nineteenth century alienated themselves from their Islamic heritage. Moreover, English education "placed an impenetrable barrier between the nineteenth century and the immediate pre-British past, which perhaps had contained certain healthy non-conformist elements along with much that was undoubtedly ossified."[12] The absence of pre British Islamic scholarship was a result of the rapid disappearance of the knowledge of Persian, and the emergence of English historiography.[13] The Indian intelligentsia became dependent on these narratives of history, as did Rammohun. This particular mind frame which we see in Rammohun, of rejecting many aspects of the Islamic past and accepting many characteristics of Western-ness, is representative of his age.

---

[11] Sarkar, *Bengal Renaissance*, p. 19.

[12] Ibid., p. 18.

[13] Ibid., p. 20.

Rammohun was well versed in Sanskrit, a scholar in his own right, and a polyglot. His personal habits were like the *bhadrolok* and yet he hankered for recognition as a shastric scholar. He was "ridiculed by the pandit establishment for imitating the outward appearance of the *ashraf* (Mughal aristocrat) which was fashionable among the *bhadrolok*; he sought scholarly recognition."[14] The *bhadroloks* were Hindus, but they were influenced by the Persianized *nawabi* culture.[15] Though Rammohun would attire himself in a *nawabi* manner, he was quite anglicized in his European habits, and could speak fluent English. He was described by the missionaries in the following manner:

> Rama-Mohana-Raya, a very rich Rarhee[sic] Brahmun of Calcutta, is a respectable Sanskrit scholar, and so well versed in Persian, that he is called Moulvee-Rama-Mohana-Raya: he also writes English with correctness and reads with ease— English, Mathematical and metaphysical works. He has published, in Bengalee, one or two philosophical works from the Sanskrit which he hopes may be useful in leading his countrymen to renounce idolatory. Europeans breakfast at his house, at a

---

[14] Bruce Carlisle Robertson, *Raja Rammohun Roy. The Father of Modern India.* (Delhi: Oxford University Press, 1999), p. 24.

[15] Till the early nineteenth century, Hindus and Muslims participated in a common elite culture, but differed in how they reacted to British presence. Muslim response was largely negative as they were losing the positions of privilege which they had enjoyed for centuries.

separate table in the English fashion; he has paid us a visit at Serampore.[16]

Rammohun was a Sanskrit scholar, who was addressed as a *maulvi*, and also conformed to the prevalent notions of caste. He had to face criticism from many regarding this contradiction between theory and practice, as evident in *Chari Prasna* (1822), printed in the *Samachar Darpan* (published by the Baptist Missionaries) to which he replied in *Chari Prasner Uttar*. He was conversant with different cultural traditions, and like his forefathers, had been given an appropriate education that would allow him to work under the Muslim rulers in Murshidabad. Eventually, with the rise of British power in India, Rammohun worked for them, and grasped the full extent of what they represented.

It was relatively easy for Rammohun to navigate between different cultural and epistemic terrains. Those living in pre-colonial, British India were participants of both Islamic and Hindu cultures. Often, this fact was elided in criticisms that were targeted at Rammohun by the self-professed upholders of Hinduism of that time. Rammohun would reply that the forefathers of the true practitioners of Hinduism had interacted intimately with the Muslims; they had served "men of an alien [Muslim] race, had used Mahomodan tooth-powder and perfume, had studied Mahomedan lore with Mahomedans, had instructed men

---

[16] Collet, *Raja Rammohun Roy*, p. 72.

of an alien faith" in the religious texts.[17] It was, in other words, impossible for anyone to have been unaffected by the different aspects of Islamic culture. Rammohun was aware that he belonged to such a multi-cultural tradition. He consciously chose to learn about the Britishers and interact with them, becoming proficient in the English language, and also about all the aspects of European civilization. There were few in early nineteenth century Calcutta who were so well versed in Hindu, Islamic and British cultures.

---

[17] Ibid., p. 150.

SECTION II:
Tohfat 'l-muwahhidin.

3 ANALYSING *TOHFAT 'L-MUWAHHIDIN.*

The *Tohfat*: Rammohun's first printed works and the realm of Persian print.

Rammohun entered the realm of print culture at a time in history when there were few native editors, writers and printers involved. That he did make use of print at a time when printed texts were still new amongst the natives reveals his capacity to absorb and make use of new technologies. His first published work, *Tohfat 'l-muwahhidin,* was in Persian—as Bengali was yet to become the language of intellectual discourse—and printed in Murshidabad around 1803, where he was working as the private *munshi* for Thomas Woodford.[18] Thomas Woodford was the registrar of the Appellate Court at Murshidabad at that time. Though it is not documented, we can assume that the presence of the British community in Murshidabad, (Baron Sir John Hedley D'Oyly , was the resident of the Company at the Court of Nawab Babar Ali of Murshidabad) meant that it had access to the technology of

---

[18] For a detailed analysis, see Bruce Carlisle Robertson, *Raja Rammohun Roy, The Father of Modern India*, pp. 24-30.

print, and a small imperial public sphere that was acquainted with it. We know little about Rammohun's intended readership, but an examination of the text makes it evident that it would have had to be a literate one, and would have been one that was familiar with an Islamic educational system. The *Tohfat* is a theological tract on monotheism and strongly condemns idolatry. In the *Tohfat*, Rammohun states that his own religion was a mix of the different religious traditions that were prevalent in India. What becomes evident is that Rammohun's education was an Islamic one and many have commented upon his style of argumentation. According to Abid U. Ghazi:

> Roy's writing is clearly that of a Madrasa stylist, naturally fluent in the use of Arabic technical and literary vocabulary acceptable in Persian. He uses Persian couplets, Qur'anic verses, and Arabic and Persian idioms to embellish his expression. Such could be acquired over years of study, training and acquaintance with all aspects of Muslim culture. … He uses the entire armory of Islamic logic to support his ideas, which themselves are ultimately turned against the tenet of all established religions, especially Islam.[19]

---

[19] Abid. U. Ghazi; cited in Robertson, *Raja Rammohun Ray*, pp. 26-28.

His subsequent theological and socio-political writings, for which we know him, reveal little influence of his knowledge of Islamic theology. Bruce Robertson states that Rammohun did not know the Upanishads at this stage in his "intellectual development," and this work is of little importance for the study of his later religion.[20] Subsequently, Rammohun educated himself in other languages and religious traditions.

What is still a matter of speculation is as to how Rammohun was able to print his works in Murshidabad. This is something we know little about. Is it possible that Rammohun sent his work to Calcutta? Did some printer carry a press to Murshidabad? Were there others involved? What was the nature of the print industry or was the text a result of a solitary printer churning out translations from Persian manuscripts? Was Rammohun able to print the *Tohfat* as a result of his intimacy with Woodford who would have known the printers in Calcutta? In fact, we know more about the realm of Persian print in Calcutta than we do about the realm of print in Murshidabad.

A parallel world of printers that catered to the needs of the Britishers existed in Calcutta; these were publishers who were printing works in Persian and other native languages, apart from also printing in English. It might be possible that Rammohun was aware of these printers through

---

[20] Robertson, *Raja Rammohun Roy*, pp. 25, 30.

Woodford, for whom he was working in Murshidabad, but we really cannot say for sure. Only Britishers would have had access to Persian fonts and the printing presses. By the late 1780s, most printing presses would have had fonts in different languages. The most well known type foundry was established by Charles Wilkins who was attached to the Honourable Company's Press. It was in Malda, where the Company's press was initially situated, and it was here that Wilkins perfected the Persian types. There were a few other foundries that established expertise in producing Oriental fonts as these types were not easily available for import from Europe. The most successful commercial foundry that was set up was by Daniel Stuart and John Cooper who supplied to the Chronicle Press.[21] By early 1787, they had produced fonts in Bengali and Persian which were used for vernacular notices in the *Calcutta Chronicle*.

The easy accessibility of fonts made it possible for the circulation of works in native languages. Natives did not feature as readers of these works that were printed in "Oriental languages." The intended readership was clearly European. The printers hoped that the fonts would encourage the natives to publish. We are not sure if Rammohun would have had contact with this group of European scholars and printers at this stage of his life. The *Tohfat*, on the other hand, was meant for an exclusive native

---

[21] For more see Graham Shaw, *Printing in Calcutta To 1800, A description and checklist of printing in late 18th century Calcutta* (London: The Bibliographical Society, 1981).pp. 29-38.

readership. This book was in keeping with other Persian writings by native scholars of this time, and most unlike the works that were printed by the Orientalist scholars.

There was a community of Britishers who, for reasons of commerce or for scholarship, was interested in bringing out printed texts in Indian languages. Francis Gladwin makes this clear in his quarterly journal, the *Asiatic Miscellany*, which he started in 1785. He wrote that the "design of the Asiatick Miscellany" would contain original works in native languages:

> Some gentlemen have promised, and others have actually supplied us with some genuine extracts from Persian authors of repute, translated with so much care, as to admit of being published with the original and translation on opposite pages. And though this part of the Work may, at first, seem particularly designed for those who study the Persian language and will undoubtedly be of singular use to them, it is yet by no means on their account alone, that the extracts appear in that form. The translations will, we trust, be always matter of curiosity and entertainment to English readers also, who in seeing them accompanied by their respective originals, will have reason to be satisfied, that what is presented to them as [a] specimen of eastern

history or composition, is neither spurious
nor disguised by borrowed ornament, but is
genuine, pure and unadulterated.[22]

Gladwin makes it clear that in his Persian writings he was
targeting a readership that was specifically non native and
interested in "unadulterated" native texts. His notion of the
public included those who were interested in Persian, and
even those Englishmen who would be "entertained" by the
"genuine, pure" fonts.

Rammohun would have been well read in the works that
were printed in Gladwin's journal;[23] but his readership for
the *Tohfat*, on the other hand, was specifically native. One
can hypothesize that his realm of readers was based in
Murshidabad, and was very literate in Islamic theology. The
realm of Persian readers that Gladwin was targeting was
very different from the realm or readers within which
Rammohun was situated. Yet, soon, the world of
Rammohun would embrace the world of Gladwin and
Rammohun would be targeting the same readers that
Gladwin was writing for. The center of power was
changing, and Rammohun was aware of this. Conforming
to the dominant Islamic worldview was no longer in
fashion. Rammohun turned his attention to writing in

---

[22] *The Asiatik Miscellany*, cited in Thankappan Nair, *A History of the Calcutta Press* (Calcutta: Firma KLM, 1987), pp. 116-117.

[23] For more on the nature of works printed in the *Asiatik Miscellenary*, and the other translated Persian works, see Nair, *A History*, pp. 117-165.

English, and soon had a readership that included officials of the East India Company, Englishmen not connected to the government, missionaries, and even readers in England and in America.

4 *Tuhfat-ul-Muwahhidin, or, A Gift to Monotheists.*

The following section is from Sophia Dobson Collet's *The Life and Letters of Raja Rammohun Roy,* ed. Dilip Kumar Biswas and Prabhat Chandra Ganguli (Calcutta: Sadharon Brahmo Samaj, 1900). Reprint 1988.

Relieved from the fear of paining his father, Rammohun soon began to make his heresies known to the world. He removed to Murshidabad, the old Moghul capital of Bengal, and there he published his first work, a treatise in Persian (with an Arabic preface), entitled *Tuhfat-ul-Muwahhidin, or, A Gift to Monotheists*. This was a bold protest against the idolatrous element in all established religions,[24]

---

[24] By a very natural mistake, the subject of this treatise was long supposed, in England, to form its actual   title, and the essay was always designated by the name **"Against the Idolatry of all Religions**." No translation of this treatise appears to have been made until quite recently, when it was rendered into English by a learned and enthusiastic Mahomedan. The full title of his pamphlet is as follows : *Tuhfat-ul-Muivah- hidin, or, A Gift to Deists*, by the late Rajah Rammohun Roy, translated into English by Moulavi Obaidullah El Obaide, Superintendent of the Dacca Government Madrassa, and published under the auspices of the Adi Brahmo Somaj, Calcutta, 1884.

the drift of the treatise being that while all religions are based on one common foundation, viz., the belief justified by the facts, in One Supreme Being who has created and sustains the whole universe, they all differ in the details of the super-structure erected thereupon, these superstructures being all equally unjustified by any basis of fact, and arising solely from the imagination of men working in vacua. The treatise bears many traces of Rammohun's Patna training, being written in an abstruse style, and abounding with Arabic logical and philosophical terms. Its arrangement is, how-ever, quite unsystematic, and the whole is merely a series of descriptive sketches; but these show much acuteness of observation and reasoning, and are pervaded by a strong tinge of that bitter earnestness which results from the long suppression of intense feeling. The author writes as though he had been obliged to stand by and witness a number of priestly impositions which he could not hinder and was prevented from exposing; and no doubt this had really been the case. The treatise is important as the earliest available expression of his mind, and as showing his eagerness to bear witness against established error but it is too immature to be worth reproducing as a whole. A few passages only are worth quoting as indications of what he was at this early period.

It may be seen that the followers of certain religions believe that the Creator has made mankind for the performance of the duties bearing on our present and future life by observing the precepts of that particular religion ; and that the followers of other religions who differ from them are liable to punishment and torment in the future life. And as the members of each particular sect defer the good results of their own acts and the bad results of their rivals' acts to the life after death none of them can refute the dogmas of others in this life. Consequently they sow the seeds of prejudice and disunion in the hearts of each other and condemn each other to the deprivation of eternal blessings whereas it is quite evident that all of them are living in the equal enjoyment of the external blessings of heaven, such as the light of the stars, the pleasure of the season of spring, the fall of rain, health of body, external and internal good, and other pleasures of life; and that all are equally liable to suffer from inconveniences and pains, such as gloomy darkness, severe cold, mental disease, narrow circumstances and other outward and inward evils, without any distinction, although following different religions.

The Brahmins have a tradition that they have strict orders from God to observe their ceremonies and hold their faith for ever. There are many injunctions to this effect in the Sanskrit language, and I, the humblest creature of God, having been born among them, have learnt the language and got those injunctions by heart; and this nation having confidence therein cannot give them up, although they have been subjected to many troubles and persecutions, and were threatened with death by the followers of Islam. The followers of Islam on the other hand, according to the purport of the holy verse of the Koran 'Kill the idolators wherever you find them, and capture the unbelievers in holy war, and after doing so either set them free by way of obligation to them or by taking ransom,' quote authority from God that killing idolators and persecuting them in every case are obligatory by divine command. Among those idolators the Brahmins, according to the Moslem belief, are the worst. Therefore the followers of Islam, excited by religious zeal, desirous to carry out the orders of God, have done their utmost to kill and persecute the polytheists and unbelievers in the prophetic mission of the Seal of Prophets Mohammed], and the blessing to the present and future worlds (may the divine benediction rest on him and his disciples). Now are these contradictory precepts or orders consistent with the wisdom and mercy of the great, generous, and disinterested Creator, or are these the fabrications of the followers of religion? I think a sound mind will not hesitate to prefer the latter alternative.

There is a saying which is often heard from teachers of different religions as an authority for their several creeds. Each of them says that his religion, which gives information about future reward or punishment after death, is either true or false. In the second case, i.e., if it be false, and there be no future reward or punishment, there is no harm in believing it to be true; while in the first case, i.e., its being true, there is a great danger for unbelievers.

The poor people who follow these expounders of religion, holding this saying to be a conclusive argument, always boast of it. The fact is that habit and training make men blind and deaf in spite of their own eyes and ears. The above saying is fallacious in two respects.

Firstly, their saying that in the second case there is no harm in believing it to be true, is not to be admitted. For to believe in the real existence of anything after obtaining proofs of such existence is possible to every individual man; but to put faith in the existence of such things as are remote from experience and repugnant to reason is not in the power of a sensible man. Secondly, the entertaining a belief in these things may become the source of various mischiefs and immoral practices, owing to gross ignorance, want of experience, bigotry, deceit, &c. And if this argument were valid, the truth of all forms of religion might be proved therefrom; for the same arguments may equally be advanced by all. Hence there would be great perplexity for a man. He must either believe all religions to be true, or adopt one and reject the others. But as the first alternative is impossible, consequently the second must be adopted and in this case he has again to make inquiries into truth and falsehood of various religions, and this is the chief object of my discourse.

The followers of different religions, seeing the paucity of the number of Monotheists in the world, sometimes boast that they are on the side of the majority. But it may be seen that the truth of a saying does not depend upon the multitude of sayers, and the non-reliability of a narration cannot result from the small numbers of its narrators. For it is admitted by the seekers of truth, that truth is to be followed although it is against the majority of the people. Moreover, to accept the proposition that the small number of the sayers leads to the invalidity of a saying, seems to be a dangerous blow to all forms of religion. For in the beginning of every religion it had a very few supporters, viz, its founder and a few sincere followers of his, . . . while the belief in only one Almighty God is the fundamental principle of every religion.

In short, men may be divided into four classes in reference to this subject,

1st. Deceivers who in order to attract the people to themselves, consciously invent doctrines of religious faith and cause disunion and trouble among men.

2nd. Deceived persons who, without inquiring into the facts, follow others.

3rd. Persons who are at the same time deceivers and deceived ; having themselves faith in the sayings of another, they induce others to follow his doctrines.

4th. Those who by the help of Almighty God are neither deceivers nor deceived.

These few short and useful sentences expressing the opinion of this humble creature of God, have been written without any regard to men of prejudice and bigotry, in the hope that persons of sound mind will look thereon with eyes of justice. I have left the details to another work of mine entitled *Manazarutul Adyan - Discussions on Various Religions*.

P. S. In order to avoid any future change in this book by copyists, I have had these few pages printed just after composition. Let it be known that the benediction pronounced in this book after the mention of prophets is merely done in imitation of the usual custom of the authors of Arabia and Ajan.

The Discussions on Various Religions above alluded to are, unhappily, no longer procurable. I conclude then it must have been in one of these that Rammohun made some rather sarcastic remarks on Mahomet, to which reference is made by several of his biographers as having excited an amount of anger against him among the Mahomedans which was a chief cause of his removing to Calcutta. In Mr. Leonard's *History of the Brahmo Samaj*, these sarcastic remarks are said to occur in the Tuhfat, but certainly no such passage is to be found there. On the other hand it is indubitable that Rammohun always retained a large amount of sympathy with Islam for the sake of its cardinal doctrine of the Unity of God, and that he warmly appreciated the good which had thence resulted in counteracting Hindu idolatry. Mr. Adam says that Rammohun "seemed always pleased to have an opportunity of defending the character and teaching of Mahomet," of whom indeed he began to write a biography which was unhappily never finished.

No copy of Rammohun's earlier work *Manazaratul Adyan* (presumably written in Persian or like the *Tuhfat* partly in Arabic and partly in Persian) alluded to in the *Tuhfat-ul-Muwahhidin* has as yet come to light. Mr. Brajendranath Banerji who had no access to the original Persian text of the *Tuhfat-ul-Muwahhidin* expressed the opinion that Rammohun never published the *Manazaratul Adyan* though he might have contemplated the writing of such a work.

5 LETTER TO LORD BENTICK ON WESTERN EDUCATION.

To

His Excellency the Right Hon'ble William Pitt,

Lord Amherst.

My Lord,

Humbly reluctant as the natives of India are to obtrude upon the notice of Government the sentiments they entertain on any public measure, there are circumstances when silence would be carrying this respectful feeling to culpable excess. The present Rulers of India, coming from a distance of many thousand miles to govern a people whose language, literature, manners, customs and ideas are almost entirely new and strange to them, cannot easily become so intimately acquainted with their real circumstances, as the natives of the country are themselves. We should therefore be guilty of a gross dereliction of duty to ourselves, and afford our Rulers just ground of complaint at our apathy, did we omit on occasions of

WHY HAS POSTCOLONIAL THEORY FORGOTTON INDIA'S PAST?

importance like the present to supply them with such accurate information as might enable them to devise and adopt measures calculated to be beneficial to the country, and thus second by our local knowledge and experience their declared benevolent intentions for its improvement.

The establishment of a new Sanskrit School in Calcutta evinces the laudable desire of Government to improve the Natives of India by Education, -- a blessing for which they must ever be grateful; and every well wisher of the human race must be desirous that the efforts made to promote it, should be guided by the most enlightened principles, so that the stream of intelligence may flow into the most useful channels.

When this Seminary of learning was proposed, we understood that the Government in England had ordered a considerable sum of money to be annually devoted to the instruction of its Indian Subjects. We were filled with sanguine hopes that this sum would be laid out in employing European Gentlemen of talents and education to instruct the natives of India in Mathematics, Natural Philosophy, Chemistry, Anatomy and other useful Sciences, which the Nations of Europe have carried to a degree of perfection that has raised them above the inhabitants of other parts of the world.

...

We now find that the Government are establishing a

Sanskrit school under Hindoo pundits to impart such knowledge as it already currently in India. this seminary (similar in character to those existing in Europe before the time of Lord Bacon) can only be expected to load the minds of youth with grammatical niceties and metaphysical distinctions of little or no practicable use to the possessors or to society. The pupils will there acquire what was known two thousands years ago, with the addition of vain and empty subtleties since produced by speculative men, such as is already commonly taught in all parts of India.

The Sanskrit language, so difficult that almost a lifetime is necessary for its perfect acquisition, is well known to have been for ages a lamentable check to the diffusion of knowledge; and the learning concealed under the almost impervious veil is far from sufficient to reward the labor of acquiring it. but if it were thought necessary to perpetuate this language for the sake of the portion of the valuable information it contains, this might be much more easily accomplished by other means than the establishment of a new Sanskrit College; for there have been always and are now numerous professors of Sanskrit in the different parts of the country, engaged in teaching this language as well as the other branches of literature which are to be the object of the new Seminary. Therefore, their more diligent cultivation, if desirable, would be effectually promoted by holding out premiums and granting certain allowances to those most eminent Professors, who have already undertaken on their own account to teach them, and would be such rewards be stimulated to still greater exertions.

From these considerations, as the sum set apart for the instruction of the Natives of India was intended by the Government in England, for the improvement of its Indian subjects, I beg leave to state with due deference to your Lordship's exalted situation, that if the plan now adopted be followed, it will completely defeat the object proposed; since no improvement can be expected from inducing young men to consume a dozen of years of the most valuable period of their lives in acquiring the niceties of Byakarun or Sanskrit grammar. ...

...

Neither can such improvement arise from such speculations as the following, which are the themes suggested by the Vedant: - In what manner is the soul absorbed into the deity? What relation does it bear to the divine essence? Nor will youths be fitted to be better members of society by the Vendantic doctrines, which teach them to believe that all visible things have no real existence; that as father, brother, etc. have no actual entity, they consequently deserve no real affection, and therefore, the sooner we escape from them and leave the world the better.

...

Again the student of the Nyaya Shastra cannot be said to have improved his mind after he has learned it into how many ideal classes the objects of the Universe re divided, and what speculative relation the soul bears to the body, the body to the soul, the eye to the ear, etc.

. . .

In order to enable your Lordship to appreciate the utility of encouraging such imaginary learning as above characterized, I beg your Lordship will be pleased to compare the state of science and literature in Europe before the time of Lord Bacon, with the progress of knowledge made since he wrote.

If it had been intended to keep the British nation in ignorance of real knowledge the Baconian philosophy would not have been allowed to displace the system of the schoolmen, which was the best calculated to perpetuate ignorance. In the same manner, the Sanskrit system of education would be best calculated to keep this country in darkness, if such had been the policy of the British Legislature. But as the improvement of the native population is the object of the Government, it will consequently promote a more liberal and enlightened system of instruction, embracing mathematics, natural philosophy, chemistry and anatomy, with other useful sciences which may be accomplished with the sum proposed by employing a few gentlemen of talents and learning educated in Europe, and providing a college furnished with the necessary books, instruments and other apparatus.

Calcutta,   I have etc.

The 11th December, 1823.

RAMMOHUN ROY

ABOUT
O$_2$pen Windows: A Feminist Resource and Research Center.

O$_2$pen Windows is a feminist research cum *adda* center, based in Bangalore, India. If it could, it would sustain itself with endless cups of tea and lots of stimulating research.

The Purpose: O$_2$pen Windows encourages research on both contemporary and historical socio-cultural issues and literary issues. These findings will subsequently be documented, archived and published as monographs and essays.

For more information, write to:
openwindows101@gmail.com.

VISIT US AT: www.aresourcecenter.wordpress.com.

www.ingramcontent.com/pod-product-compliance
Lightning Source LLC
Chambersburg PA
CBHW060630030426
42337CB00018B/3280